My First Book Parrot

Amazing Animals Children's Picture Books

By Molly Davidson

Mendon Cottage Books

JD-Biz Publishing

Download Free Books!

http://MendonCottageBooks.com

All Rights Reserved.

No part of this publication may be reproduced in any form or by any means, including scanning, photocopying, or otherwise without prior written permission from JD-Biz Corp and http://AmazingAnimalBooks.com. Copyright © 2015

All Images Licensed by Fotolia, Pixabay, and 123RF

Read More Amazing Animal Books

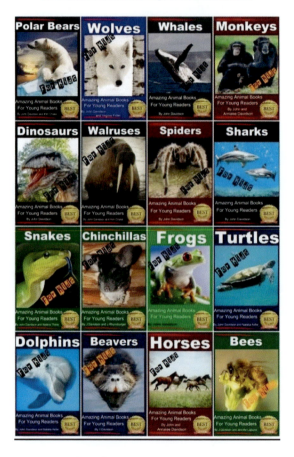

Purchase at Amazon.com

Download Free Books!

http://MendonCottageBooks.com

Table of Contents

Introduction..4

About Parrots 5

Features of Parrots 8

Where parrots live...10

What a Parrot Eats 11

Parrots are Smart...14

Parrots as Pets 17

Love Birds..19

Parakeets 21

Cockatiels...23

Cockatoos...25

African Greys..28

Macaws 30

Parrots in various cultures 33

Saving the parrots 35

Fun facts about parrots....................................37

Publisher 45

Introduction

If you want to watch birds, parrots are one of the best, because of their bright colors and loud voices.

Parrots are one of the only birds that can "talk" like a human.

About Parrots

Parrots live in the tropics, mostly in Australia, Central and South America.

Some parrots can live up to 75 years in the wild.

Parrots live in large flocks, and talk to each other very loudly with squawks and screeches.

Parrots are a very smart bird, they can be trained to do tricks and copy what their owner says.

A pair of white fronted Amazon parrots in Guanacaste, Costa Rica. Steve Jurvetson © Wikimedia Commons

Parrots live in various places, some build nests, other live in a hole of a tree, in an underground tunnel, or even in termite mounds.

Features of Parrots

Parrots weigh only 1 - 3.5 pounds, and stand about 3 feet tall.

Parrots can see and hear very well, this helps keep them out of danger.

They have four toes, two face forward and two backward, this helps them hold on tight to trees.

Their beak is very sharp and pointed; it is used for cracking open nuts and hard shells.

Where parrots live

Parrots like warm weather, this is why they live in the tropics.

Many live in the rain forest.

Some parrot species migrate in the winter and some stay in one place.

What a Parrot Eats

A parrot eats fruits, seeds, pollen, buds, nectar, nuts, and insects.

One of a parrot's favorite foods is nectar from fruit.

Gold-winged Parakeets prey on water snails, and cockatoos eat grubs.

White Cockatoo © Wikimedia Commons

Macaws and cockatoos have extra sharp beaks so they can break open nuts to get to the seeds.

They have to be careful many seeds are poisonous.

To help the food digest in their stomachs they will eat clay.

Parrots are Smart

African Grey Parrots are the best at copying sounds made by their owners.

The Amazon Parrot is known to copy sounds of other birds, not just parrots.

Parrots do not have vocal cords like humans; to make sounds they blow air through a chamber called a syrinx.

Parrots do have a tongue, this helps form the sounds, just like a human tongue does.

Parrots as Pets

Parrots are a great choice for a pet; they are the third most popular pet in America.

You will need to love and care for your parrot, be careful they will bite, if they feel like they are in danger, and it will hurt.

Parrots need big cages, and they like to have toys in them to play with.

Pet parrots have learned to sing music, dance, and even learn when their owners are happy or sad.

Love Birds

Lovebirds are cute and small; they only weigh 3.5 ounces (less than 1/4 of a pound).

They live about 10 - 15 years.

When a group of love birds are together they like to snuggle, nice and tight.

They like to perch on your shoulder; they will even spin and hang off their toys.

Love birds can live happily by themselves or with others.

Parakeets

The word parakeet means long tail.

Parakeets are great at whistling.

They love to splash in water, hang off tree branches (or toys, if they are a pet), and climb.

In the wild, parakeets will search for food when it is cool, like the mornings, and they will hang out in the shade during the hot part of the day.

Most wild parakeets live in New Zealand.

Cockatiels

Cockatiels are small parrots from Australia.

Cockatiels are cuddly, kind, and easy to train.

They are very good at whistling, and boy cockatiels can even learn to talk.

They can be many colors like yellow, silver, pearl, and red-ish brown.

If cockatiels get too bored or lonely they will start plucking their feathers out.

Cockatoos

Cockatoos are easy to pick out, they have a crest of feathers above their head, which can be raised or lowered at any time.

There are many species of cockatoos, some are small and some are as tall as 2 feet.

Cockatoos can live up to 80 years!

Cockatoos need lots of love and attention from their owners, or they will get sick from being so sad.

They are very loud and get excited easily; but they do not copy words and sounds of humans.

In the wild a cockatoo will raise its crest to ward off predators.

African Greys

African Greys have grey feathers, like their name, and a strong black beak.

African Grey are the smartest parrot, they are good at copying sounds and learning new tricks fast.

If you get one as a pet they will copy household sounds, like the vacuum, washing machine, dogs, and of course, humans.

Macaws

Macaws have beautiful, colorful, feathers.

They are the largest among all the parrots.

They have big, black, hooked beaks, which they use for cracking open nuts and fruit.

Macaws' wings are long and pointed; this helps them fly very fast.

Macaws are very loud, screechy, birds, but they are very good at copying human sounds.

If they are taken care of, and given proper nutrition, macaws can live to be 50 years old!

Parrots in various cultures

Parrot feathers were used for decorations and in cultural ceremonies.

Many years ago in Peru, parrots were worshipped by the Moche people and were used in lots of art.

The national bird of St. Vincent, an island off the coast of Venezuela, is the parrot.

Saving the parrots

There are more endangered parrots than any other bird.

There are many reasons why parrots are becoming extinct; they are losing where they live, the rainforest.

In some places, parrots are hunted for their feathers and to eat.

A group called the World Parrot Trust is trying to help save parrots.

Fun facts about parrots

King Henry VIII, Winston Churchill, Napoleon, and President Andrew Jackson all had parrots as pets.

The smallest parrot is the Pacific Parrotlet and the largest is the Hyacinth macaw.

When a parrot wags its tail, it's like when a human giggles.

Cockatoos move their heads up and down or wiggle their tongues if they are happy.

Download Free Books!

http://MendonCottageBooks.com

Purchase at Amazon.com

Website http://AmazingAnimalBooks.com

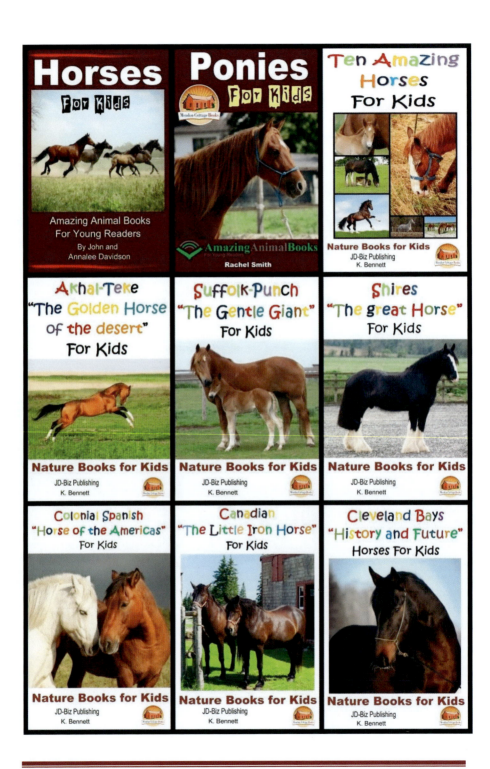

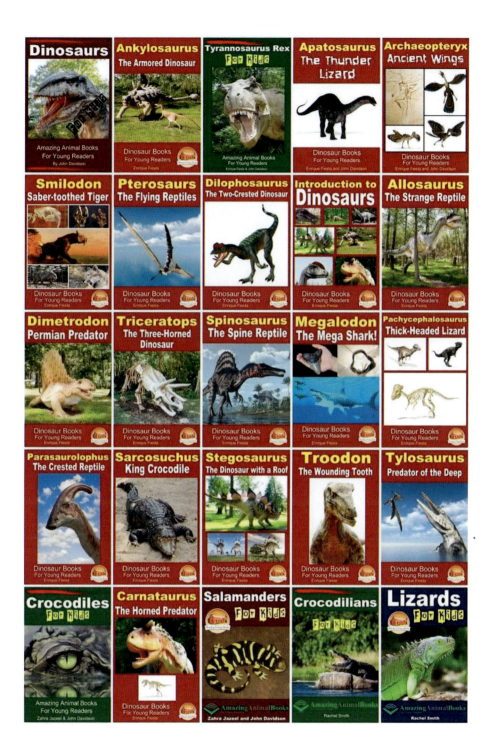

My First Book about Parrots · Page 41

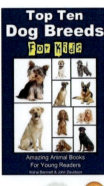

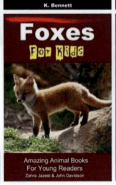

Our books are available at

1. Amazon.com

2. Barnes and Noble

3. Itunes

4. Kobo

5. Smashwords

6. Google Play Books

Download Free Books!

http://MendonCottageBooks.com

Publisher

JD-Biz Corp

P O Box 374

Mendon, Utah 84325

http://www.jd-biz.com/

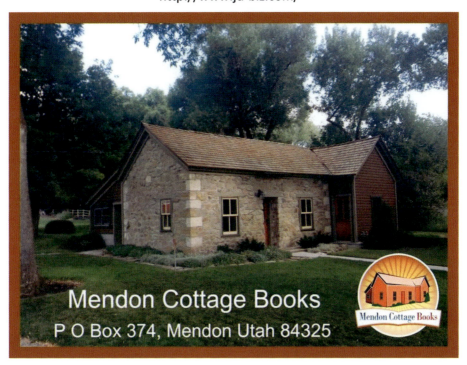

Printed in Great Britain
by Amazon